Making a Magnificent You

And the Role of Fruits and Vegetables

written by
Martin Katz, MD

This book is dedicated to my family

Thank you God for providing these Amazing, Enriching, Incredible, Optimal, and Useful foods for OUR HEALTH.

"I will give thanks to You, because I am awesomely and wonderfully *made...*"
–Psalm 139:14 NASB

Thank you to all little and big farmers, for growing the food we love to eat!

See how many tractors you can find in this book!

Copyright © 2022 by Martin Katz, MD

Published in 2022 by Fidelis Publishing, Sterling, VA-Nashville, TN

Cover and interior design and illustration by Diana Lawrence
Source imagery- 123rf

For bulk purchases, contact BulkBooks.com, call 1-888-959-5153 or email - cs@bulkbooks.com

ISBN: 978-19564-5410-9

Scripture reference is taken from the New American Standard Bible®,
Copyright © 1960, 1971, 1977, 1995, 2020 by The Lockman Foundation. All rights reserved.

Printed in the United States of America in April 2022

1 2 3 4 5 6 7 8 9 10

Y__ _r_

_ncr_d_bly

_w_s_m_!!

What does
this message
mean?

Here's a clue:
It's what you
can be!

By communicating.
Just like we love to talk to
you, your trillions of cells,
(that's 1.000.000.000),
like to talk to each other.

AND,
they need
YOUR help.

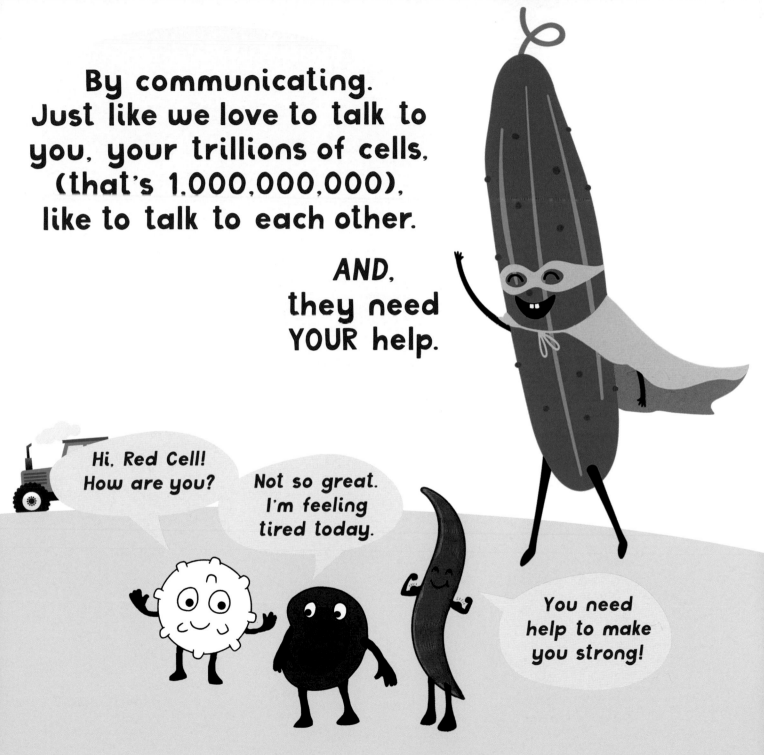

Hi, Red Cell!
How are you?

Not so great.
I'm feeling
tired today.

You need
help to make
you strong!

How can we help make that happen?!?! By eating the right foods— and that means *LOTS* of fruits and veggies!!

date
Increase your play time with your mates, eat a few dates.

apple
An apple a day keeps the doctor away.

avocado
Give me some guac, before I go into shock!! Holy moly, get me some guacamole!

arugula
Keeps the blood pumping through the jugular.

kale
Present your cells with some kale, it's your get-out-of-unhealthy-jail-bail.

asparagus
Don't be making a fuss, just eat your asparagus!

So when you eat these foods, many cells start to understand each other better!

And look what
happens to your
sentence:

Y__ __ ar_
_ncr_d_bly
aw_s_m_ !!

Keep eating the good stuff like:

eggplant
Please ask your aunt to cook some eggplant.

edamame
Satisfy your tummay, eat some edamame.

elderberry
It is definitely necessary to eat your elderberry.

escarole
Add some escarole to achieve your health goal.

pepper
As a meal prepper, think about adding a delicious bell pepper.

endive
Give me a high five while eating your endive.

9

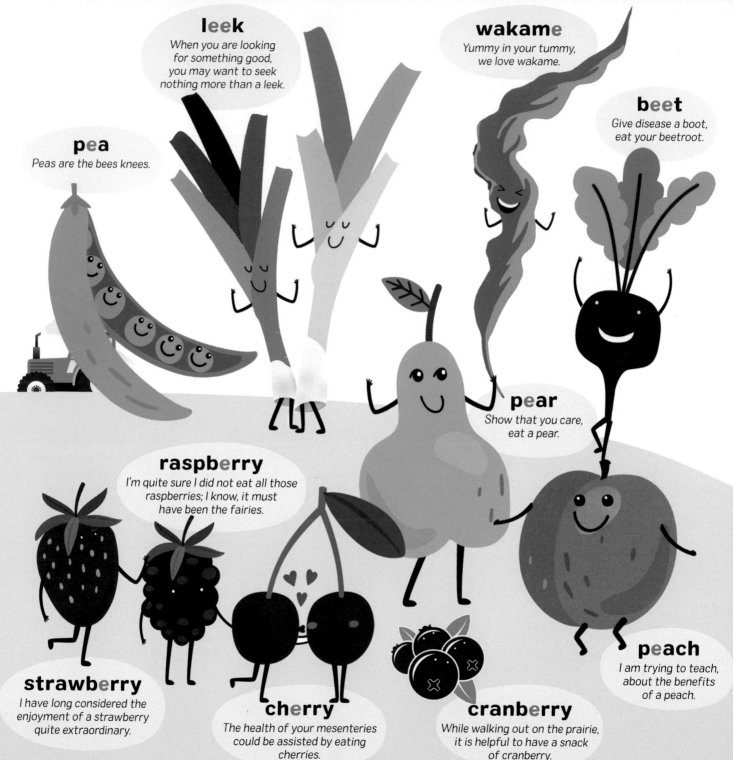

And look, your
understanding grows:

Y__ are
_ncred_bly
awes_me!!

and your cells
are thankful!!

So many more amazing foods to keep you going strong:

kiwi
"Oiu Oiu", I love me some kiwi!

iceberg lettuce
Please provide for us some of that crunchy Iceberg lettuce.

Indian squash
People like to nosh on some squash.

pineapple
you don't have to grapple with eating a pineapple.

12

spinach

Enjoy a bowl of spinach while playing a game of cribbage.

garlic

Garlic is what you should pick should you start feeling sick.

lime

For sailors to continue in their prime, they should enjoy an occasional lime.

fig

You'll feel like you're in the "bigs" when you eat your figs.

radish

Your parents may get madish if you don't eat your radish.

nectarine

All kings and queens enjoy the refreshing taste of nectarines.

The message is definitely clearer. Do you have it?

Y_ _ are incredibly awes_me!!

If not, keep it going. You are so close! Your cells are loving it: being bathed in all that goodness.

And here's more:

kohlrabi
Eat some Kolhrabi with your Wasabi.

broccoli
Broccoli is a vegetable you can trust, to consume it is an absolute must.

orange
Oranges are nutritious and delicious.

corn
Do not let another day dawn until you have had the sweet taste of grilled corn.

olive
I love a juicy olive.

carrot
The great feeling of being granted a merit can come from eating a crunchy carrot.

onion
Try rubbing an onion on your bunion; may help, or make you yelp.

15

radicchio
If you are moving really slow, perk up your day with some radicchio.

pomegranate
Could there be anything better on this planet than the pleasure of eating a pomegranate?

potato
How would tornadoes affect a patch of potatoes?

longan
If you are Tongan, do you like longan?

lemon
Even though lemons are sour, they can be quite tempting to devour.

tangelo
While playing a cello, reach out for the great taste of a tangelo.

tomato
Create with Play-Doh while eating a tomato.

okra
Something about okra that is not odd, it is a flowering plant seed pod.

carambola
You don't have to be from Hispaniola to enjoy some carambola.

collard green
Don't be like my rebellious teens; eat your collard greens.

mango
Two great things: the fun of the tango, and the enjoyment of a mango.

watermelon
Remember that guy Magellan, he may have been in search of some watermelon.

feijoa
When in Hawaii you say Aloha, when in Brazil you eat Feijoa.

We are so close now:

Yo_ are incredibly awesome!!

You are helping to get the message across!!

With just a little
more intake of goodness,
you and your cells will
have it for sure.

blueberry
It's really not scary
to enjoy a blueberry.

zucchini
Don't be a weanie;
eat your zucchini.

pumpkin
Don't be a country bumpkin,
eat up your pumpkin.

ugli fruit
No need to dispute, instead sit
back and share an ugli fruit.

mushroom
I encourage you to consume
so many more than one type
of mushroom.

prune
Enjoy your afternoons
while eating some prunes.

plum
Instead of chewing gum,
eat a nice, juicy plum.

yuca
You're in "lucka",
when you eat your yuca.

cucumber
Good nutrition should always be
your number, so eat a cucumber.

rutabaga
Nothing quite like a well built
Studebaker, unless you are considering
eating a rutabaga.

turnip
Learn up
about the turnip.

brussels sprout
Your overall health will improve no doubt,
when you consume the almighty brussel sprout.

kumquat
If you get tired of doing a squat,
eat a kumquat.

guava
A guava can be enjoyed
with a cup of java.

Very few have all five vowels:

cauliflower
Please don't underestimate the power of consuming cauliflower.

Jerusalem artichoke
Your health ain't broke when you eat a Jerusalem artichoke.

In fact, most only have two vowels. But if you eat a good variety of fruit and veggies you'll get *all* the vowels!

Now you can make total sense of what was being said.

You are incredibly awesome!!

You got it,
your cells get it.

Let's keep it that way.
Eat all the goodness that is out there and stay away from the junk.

Now you just need to make sure you keep it up with (fill in the blanks):

_x_rc_s_, sl__p,
dr_nk_ng w_t_r,
t_m_ __td__rs,
and t_m_ with
fr__nds and f_m_ly.*

Hard to read, hard to understand. Make it easy by eating your fruits and veggies and soon you will see that all of this is important!

*Exercise, sleep, drinking water, time outdoors, and time with friends and family.

You're doing great! You just learned all these fruits and veggies by their vowels. Now let's find out more about them!

FRUITS

apple
avocado
banana
blueberry
carambola
cherry
cranberry
date
elderberry
feijoa
fig
grape
guava
kiwi
kumquat
lemon
lime
longan

mango
nectarine
orange
papaya
peach
pear
pineapple
plum
pomegranate
prune
pumpkin
raisin
raspberry
strawberry
tangelo
ugli fruit
watermelon

VEGGIES

arugula
asparagus
beet
broccoli
brussels sprout
cabbage
carrot
cauliflower
cucumber
collard green
corn
edamame
eggplant
endive
escarole
garlic
iceberg lettuce
indian squash
Jerusalem
  artichoke
kale

kohlrabi
leek
malanga
mushroom
okra
olive
onion
pea
pepper
potato
radicchio
radish
rutabaga
spinach
tomato
turnip
wakame
yam
yuca
zucchini

Hmmm... am I a fruit or veggie??

24

FUN FACTS about FRUITS and VEGGIES

Glycemic load: Low: <10   Medium: 11–19   High: >20

APPLE: Found all over the world, but originally from Central Asia. Comes in all shapes and sizes—a fun, delicious, filling fruit. Contains numerous beneficial antioxidants and nutrients such as quercetin, as well as vitamin C and fiber. Keeps constipation at bay. Bobbing for apples? Twenty-five percent of an apple's volume is air, which is why they float. *"Millions saw the apple fall, but Newton was the one that asked why."* —Bernard Baruch
• Glycemic load: 5

ARUGULA: Tender leaves and a tangy taste; part of the incredible cruciferous vegetable family. Arugula has been cultivated in the Mediterranean area since Roman times, and has been mentioned in the Old Testament as "Oroth." Provides beneficial nitrates and polyphenols, which have been shown to enhance athletic performance, control blood pressure, and keep you healthy. That's right, you can run faster and further while staying well.
• Glycemic load: 1

ASPARAGUS: Hopefully your mother ate a lot of this while you were in the womb, as it is very high in folate, which is incredibly important for normal cell growth. Don't be surprised by the funny smell it can give your urine, but instead, enjoy all the health benefits it can provide after eating it. Everybody makes "asparagus pee," not everyone can smell it, a relative "anosmia."
• Glycemic load: 3

AVOCADO: An incredibly nutritious fruit—yes, fruit—known more for its fat and potassium content (21 grams of fat) than sugar content (1 gram, with 12.8 grams of carbohydrates). Good source of vitamins B, C, E, and K, fiber (10 gm/serving), and potassium (727 mg). The name "avocado" originated from the Aztec word ahuacatl, which means "testicle."
• Glycemic load: 3

BANANA: Although fairly high in sugar, bananas are a great source of fiber, a prebiotic known as inulin, potassium, vitamin B6, and manganese. Unripe bananas can also provide resistant starch, another prebiotic. Next time you get an itchy insect bite, rub the inside of a banana peel against your skin until it turns brown and feel the itch melt away.
• Glycemic load: 18

BEET: One of my favorites, due to helping with blood flow and athletic performance. Beware, if you eat a lot, it can make it look like there is blood in your urine or poop, called beeturia. It contains a high amount of nitrates, which can be converted in the body to a beneficial compound called nitric oxide. High in nutrients, fiber, minerals, and vitamins.. Enjoy in a salad, or even mixed into your favorite brownie mix. America's third president, Thomas Jefferson, had beetroots grown in his gardens at his beautiful home Monticello in Virginia, close to where I live.
• Glycemic load: 5

BLUEBERRY: A food index scoring system, Aggregate Nutrient Density Index (ANDI), places blueberries near the top due to their density of bioactive compounds shown to contribute to an individual's health. Great on cereal, waffles, yogurt, oatmeal, or in a smoothie or salad, this tasty, nutritious fruit is a great addition to your meal. Hailed as a "superfood," blueberries are one of the few fruit native to North America. If all the blueberries grown in North America in one year were spread out in a single layer, they would cover a four lane highway from New York to Chicago.
• Glycemic load: 6

BROCCOLI: Considered a superfood, broccoli is rich in vitamins, minerals, and antioxidants. Part of the cruciferous family, long studied to be very beneficial in numerous health concerns and diseases. Lightly steaming broccoli is the best way to cook it while maintaining its nutritional content. Broccoli is on the Environmental Working Group's list of "Clean 15," meaning it has a lower pesticide risk. Some friends and I started a supplement company around broccoli because it is the "Crown Jewel of Nutrition" - www.mara-labs.com.
• Glycemic load: 3 (raw)

BRUSSELS SPROUT: A true cruciferous vegetable family resemblance, brussels sprouts appear like a miniature cabbage. Packed with beneficial antioxidants, this is a food you should learn how to cook so it is an appealing addition to your diet. Please explore ways to cook brussels sprouts, whether with balsamic vinegar, hollandaise sauce, butter, or bacon. Just don't overcook, as this is where they lose their more pleasant flavor. In addition to vitamins and minerals, it is one of the best plant sources of a beneficial amount of omega 3 fatty acid.
• Glycemic load: 3

CABBAGE: Skip the bread, make a sandwich using these delicious, nutritious leaves. A very beneficial member of the cruciferous family. So many compounds shown to help in numerous ways, you should eat it in green, purple, or red. Russia consumes more than four times the amount of cabbage compared to the next closest country.
• Glycemic load: 2

CARAMBOLA: Branch out and try this "star fruit" which is gaining in popularity. I give it five stars for the high nutrient content in this plant, shown in mice studies to be very helpful in limiting disease. Because of its sweet and sour taste it is quite versatile in recipes. Described as having a complicated flavor, compared to pineapple, plum, and lemon.
• Glycemic load: 3

CARROT: A great snack wherever you are: on a hike, bike, road trip, or at your desk. Not only tasty and crunchy, they come in a bunch of fun colors and are also nutritionally great for you. If you need vitamin K, potassium, biotin, fiber, and especially vitamin A, this is a great go-to food. And it has been shown to support your eye health. Reportedly, the voice of Bugs Bunny, Mel Blanc, did not like carrots, despite Bugs Bunny saying: "Carrots are divine . . . You get a dozen for a dime, It's maaaa-gic!"
• Glycemic load: 3

CAULIFLOWER: Known as a nutrition superstar, this is one versatile cruciferous veggie. Used as a potato, rice, or even pizza crust substitute. Low in calories, yet containing most of the vitamins you need, fiber, and beneficial antioxidants. Also rich in choline and sulforaphane precursors, two beneficial plant compounds to help you stay healthy. If white cauliflower is too bland, try the green, purple, or orange variety, or the fascinating and beautiful Romanesco cauliflower.
• Glycemic load: 2

CHERRY: Not just a sweet fruit, this food is packed with phytonutrients found to be beneficial in reducing gout, soreness after exercise, heart disease, cancer, and even your memory as you age. But don't eat the pit or the fruit if the pit has been crushed. Good source of fiber, potassium, manganese, and vitamin C. An average cherry tree yields 7,000 cherries, enough to make twenty-eight cherry pies.
• Glycemic load: 7

COLLARD GREEN: Another cruciferous, a family known for its nutrients, not its calories. Clinical studies on fruits and vegetables, and specifically cruciferous vegetables, demonstrate an inverse relationship between chronic diseases and consumption. Collards provide all these benefits, as well as a healthy dose of vitamin A, calcium, vitamin K, iron, vitamin C, and magnesium. Collards are known to be tastier and more nutritious in the colder months, after the first frost.
• Glycemic load: 1

CORN: While nutritionally valuable, corn does tend to raise blood sugar as it is a starch vegetable (high in carbohydrates). So while it pains me to say it (because eating corn off the cob is just so fun and delicious), if you have a blood sugar problem/insulin resistance, you may want to limit this vegetable. Corn always has an even number of rows, generally 16, containing 800 kernels. The vast majority of corn grown in the United States, approximately 92 percent, is genetically modified! And most of it is used to feed animals.
• Glycemic load: 11

CRANBERRY: A staple of Thanksgiving, but due to their nutritional value, should be consumed more often. Women know of their benefit to help limit or prevent urinary tract infections, but these little goodies also offer a great variety of phytonutrients that may help the immune

system, prevent heart disease, and possibly even cancer. Also high in fiber, vitamin C, and manganese, as well as vitamins E and K. Despite the commercials, cranberries are not grown in water, but instead are flooded while on the vine so they float and can be more easily harvested.
• Glycemic load: 2

CUCUMBER: From beauty products to kitchen, this fruit has been proven to be a good addition to a healthy approach to living. Due to its high water content, cucumbers should be enjoyed on a hot day. Cucumbers also contain many very beneficial triterpenes, flavonoids, and other nutrients beneficial to the skin. *"Cool as a cucumber"* was first used as a phrase in the poem "A New Song" by English poet John Gay in 1732.
• Glycemic load: 1

DATE: Due to being high in natural sugar, as well as a good source of potassium and polyphenols, dates are my favorite on-the-go snack. For longer runs, rides, or hikes, easy to carry, convenient, and delicious. Use dates to make energy snacks, or use them in salads, smoothies, or Mediterranean stews. Dates were one of the first cultivated trees, used for food, making wine, or as a symbol of victory.
• Glycemic load (1 pitted date): 3. 1 ounce: 11

EDAMAME: Can be great as a prepared side dish or snack. High in fiber, vitamin K, folate, and protein, with decent amounts of calcium, iron, choline, it's very close to a complete food source. Consider growing your own or buying locally. According to the USDA in 2012, 93 percent of all soy was genetically modified to be resistant to the herbicide glyphosate. Edamame means "beans on branches," and are really immature soybeans, so please ensure they are sourced well.
• Glycemic load: 4

EGGPLANT: Belongs to the nightshade family, however, by definition a fruit. Comes in a variety of colors and is versatile in the kitchen. Very good source of fiber, and antho-cyanins—a chemical that helps protect against cell damage. So many delightful preparations for eggplant: can you say baba ghanoush or eggplant lasagna? Eggplant is richer in nicotine than any other edible plant, a beneficial plant compound, just absolutely not in the form of a cigarette or vape.
• Glycemic Load: 1

ELDERBERRY: A source of nutrition and medicine for thousands of years. Can be used as a brew, or cooked and eaten like a fruit, some evidence suggests this berry, packed with vitamin C, can limit the effect of the common cold or flu on your body. The dark pigment of the fruit also provides powerful antioxidants. Cook them and combine them with your favor-ite berries to create a delicious and nutritious pie.
• Glycemic load: 5

ENDIVE: Part of the bitter-leaf vegetable or chicory family, full of flavor and fiber, known for its prebiotic properties. Also a great source of vitamins A, K, folate, potassium, manga-nese, and healthy phytonutrients. Endive can be lightly cooked to enhance the nutty flavor and decrease the bitter, or used in salads, or as a "boat" for appetizers such as guacamole or salsa. Culturally in America, endives are con-sidered gourmet and therefore higher in cost. Across the Atlantic in France, it is a common winter and spring vegetable and therefore less expensive.
• Glycemic Load: 1

ESCAROLE: Considered part of the chicory family, and therefore closely related to endive. Provides a lot of the same benefits, but consid-ered not quite as complete a food. Cooking it will mellow out the bitter outer leaves, but the inner leaves are more tender and sweeter. If you enjoy Italian foods, this green will often be used in recipes.
• Glycemic load: low

FEIJOA: Known as pineapple guava, two of my favorites, this fruit is certainly tropical, and delicious. Packed with folate, vitamins B and C, as well as mineral manganese, copper, and mag-nesium, it is also nutritious. Great fiber content as the whole fruit can be consumed, though the skin is generally discarded. Can be eaten raw or in numerous different presentations or squeezed to enjoy as a juice. Easy to grow and, unless you live in high humidity, should be con-sidered if you live in Hardiness Zones 8–11 (www. arborday.org/media/zones.cfm).
• Glycemic load: 10

FIG: One of my favorite snacks on a longer bike ride, figs are sweet and nutritious. Due to their sweetness, they can be used as sugar alternatives as well as in jams or desserts. A great source of vitamins, especially the B's, as well as potassium, and magnesium. They also help to prevent diseases due to their rich content of phytochemicals. Keep these in your diet, especially if you show symptoms of irrita-ble bowel syndrome, constipation prominent. Known as the "fruit of the gods," figs contain the highest percentage of sugar content of any fruit.
• Glycemic load: 4 (1 large fig)

GARLIC: Used in kitchens across the world for its incredible taste, but in years past, garlic was primarily used for medicinal purposes. Today garlic has been found to be beneficial for fighting the common cold, reducing the risk of cancer and dementia, improving bone health, and even lowering your risk of heart disease. High in vitamin B6, calcium, manganese, sele-nium, and other minerals. Likely made popular as a repellent in *Dracula* due to its use as a mosquito repellent (another blood sucker).
• Glycemic load: 1 (3 cloves)

GRAPE: A favorite finger food, just ensure cutting them into smaller pieces for our younger children, and older adults should they have a swallowing problem. They come in numerous colors, with the darker red and black having a higher phytonutrient count, with the presence of resveratrol, shown in many studies to have many health benefits. Due to the combination of vitamins, fiber, minerals, and antioxidants, this is a great choice to curb sugar cravings without increasing the risk of diabetes. Higher on the list of the EWG list of pesticide foods, so please thoroughly wash your grapes or consider buying organic.
• Glycemic load: 9

GUAVA: Look no further if you seek a delicious, filling, low-calorie snack packed with vitamins, nutrients, and vitamin C. Not only is the fruit good for supporting your health, but the leaf extract has also been shown to be beneficial. A better source of vitamin C than an orange.
• Glycemic load: 2 (1 fruit)

ICEBERG LETTUCE: Crunchy and mild in flavor, this variety of lettuce can be a great way to introduce kids to eating greens. Despite not packing the same punch as the darker greens, iceberg lettuce does provide some beneficial minerals and vitamins, as well as being high in water content and relatively high in fiber. There are two classes of lettuce heads: crisp or butter. Iceberg lettuce is a crisp-head type, brittle textured leaves that form a hard head.
• Glycemic load: 1

INDIAN SQUASH: Contains some vitamins, minerals, but has a large amount of water, so can be quite hydrating. Many varieties of squash are incredibly nutritious, so be sure to include these varieties when cooking squash. A versatile food in the kitchen, it can be used in many conventional and ethnic dishes.
• Glycemic load: 2

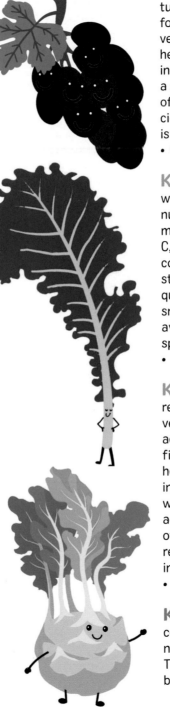

JERUSALEM ARTICHOKE: Neither from Jerusalem, nor an artichoke, this is a tuber more closely resembling ginger. Good for iron, vitamins B and C, and, like so many vegetables, the fiber content helps support the health of the gastrointestinal tract. Consume in a similar manner to potatoes, thinly sliced in a salad, or fermented to decrease the amount of gas you may produce. Nutritious and delicious, it's the vegetable you can trust, eating it is a must.
• Glycemic load: 11

KALE: Due to being low-calorie yet packed with antioxidants, kale is among the most nutrient dense foods on the planet. High in minerals, and nutrients, especially vitamins A, C, and K. Kale contains some of my favorite compounds, well known for helping the body stay healthy, such as sulforaphane precursors, quercetin, and indole-3-carbinol. A favorite snack, kale chips: just drizzle on some olive or avocado oil, salt, and your favorite herbs and spices, bake and enjoy.
• Glycemic load: 3

KOHLRABI: Slightly sweeter than its relatives broccoli and cabbage, this versatile vegetable is gaining popularity in kitchens across the country. Extraordinarily high in fiber, this cruciferous vegetable is great for gut health. And just like its relatives, it too is high in nutritional value. Available locally during the winter months, it can be eaten raw as a snack, added to salads, or cooked, sauteed for use in other dishes. The largest kohlrabi grown was a record breaker at the Alaskan State Fair, coming in at a whopping 96lbs 15oz.
• Glycemic load: 3

KUMQUAT: This delicious fruit should be consumed whole, with lots of beneficial phytonutrients and flavonoids coming from the peel. The peel also contains essential oils which are beneficial to health. Can be used in garnishes,

chutneys, marmalades, sliced in salads or many other uses. Unlike other fruits, the sweetness comes from the peel, tartness from the juice.
• Glycemic load: 1

LEEK: *"Ah! There's a 'leek' in the boat"—Cloudy with a Chance of Meatballs.* Leeks are a food not only good for lines in a movie, but their sweeter taste (compared to veggies in the same family) and creamier texture in sauces are quite versatile in the kitchen. Full of plant compounds such as allicin, kaempferol, and thiosulfinates (easy for you to say) which have been shown to support the body through numerous disease processes. Leeks can be added to just about any dish, dip, soup, sauce, or salad.
• Glycemic load: 5

LEMON: Seldom eaten alone, but certainly can contribute to many meals, and the basis of lemonade. Lemon is also used as an essential oil for many conceived benefits. Due to being hybridized from limes (and citron), they share many common benefits, high vitamin C being one of them. Squeezing half a lemon into your water every day, can not only make it more enticing to drink, but may come with some health benefits. Lemons, once presented to kings as a gift due to being rare, are picked from the tree all year round, producing approximately 500–600 pounds of fruit.
• Glycemic load: 4

LIME: There's a reason Brits are called "Limeys"—a doctor figured that giving sailors lime juice would limit the effects of scurvy: bleeding gum disease, swollen joints, exhaustion. Scurvy is from low vitamin C, which limes happen to have a lot of. They also contain other nutrients and protective molecules that can help build immunity, promote healthy skin, and even prevent kidney stones. Limes can be used for making Paddington Bear's favorite: marmalade.
• Glycemic load: 1

LONGAN: Longan and lychee, lychee or longan. Very similar, both similar in calorie, high in vitamin C. Both contain a good amount of polyphenols—used in Chinese medicine for liver and pancreatic health, some minerals, and even some B vitamins. Also, contain a good amount of fiber to improve the health of your bowel. With transparent flesh and a dark pupil-like seed, the fruit appears like an eyeball, known as "Dragon's Eye."
• Glycemic load: 10

MALANGA: High in fiber, and nutrient dense. High source of potassium, and B vitamins, can be a great flour alternative, certainly if you are gluten allergic/sensitive. Try it in Puerto Rican or Cuban dishes or to thicken your sauces or soup. Add spices, oil, and bake to make "fries." If you tend toward food allergies, consider malanga, thought to be one of the more hypoallergenic foods available.
• Glycemic load: low

MANGO: Mmm, mmm mangoes, certainly one of my favorite fruits, and full of nutrients. It is high in vitamins, especially C, and is also packed with numerous antioxidants. High in fiber and can also aid in digestion, making this a fruit you should include on your menu—fresh in a salad, salsa, or a smoothie. Want to tell someone you want to be their friend, given them a basket of mangoes.
• Glycemic load: 8

MUSHROOM: With books like *Healing Mushrooms*, you realize you are dealing with an incredible food. Amazingly diverse, with lots of nutritional value and antioxidants, I strongly encourage you to try all varieties available in this country, about seven of the 2,000 edible mushrooms; possibly more at local farmer's markets. The only non-fortified vegetable food that contains vitamin D. Please do not hunt for these unless you know what you are doing—they can be toxic.
• Glycemic load: 2

NECTARINE: You may be able to substitute for peaches in recipes, but these two fruits differ. Nectarines have a thinner, smoother skin, while peaches have "fuzz." The fruit is often firmer and sometimes sweeter than peaches—give them a try and see which you prefer. You can't go wrong, as they are both packed with vitamins A, C, E, niacin, and minerals copper, manganese, potassium, and phosphorus, as well as a good amount of fiber. Similar to peaches, plums, apricots, and cherries, nectarines are known as "stone fruit" due to the hard pit surrounding the seed.
• Glycemic load: 5

OLIVE: A major part of the proven healthy Mediterranean diet, which is rich in veggies, fruits, and healthy fats. The major oil is from olives. This healthy stone fruit is packed with vitamin E, copper, iron, and calcium, as well as significant plant compounds which help to fight disease. Savory and delicious as a meal or appetizer, regardless what diet you are following. Likely due to the biblical story of Noah's ark and the dove bringing back an olive branch (a symbol of goodwill), it is featured on numerous nation's flags, multiple U.S. state flags, and the flag of the United Nations.
• Glycemic load: 1

OKRA: Known as "lady's fingers," this plant is grown in warmer, more tropical regions around the world and is a popular dish in Egypt and Louisiana. Low in calories, yet packed with goodness, including a wide range of vitamins and minerals, as well as a higher ratio of protein. Can also be quite helpful with digestion and limiting constipation. The slimy nature of this fruit can be quite useful for improving the consistency of stews, even treating hair and skin, but don't wait until it gets too old, as this is when it is used to make paper and rope.
• Glycemic load: 2

ONION: This vegetable makes me cry—with joy—for all the health benefits associated with its consumption. Onions are high in vitamin C, folate, vitamin B6, manganese, as well as protective organosulfurs and quercetin that helps to maintain your health. Also high in inulin which is a great prebiotic to feed your good gut bacteria. Can be sweet to spicy, and therefore can be used in a wide variety of cuisines.
To cut down on the crying, cut the onion while cold, like frozen, and the root end last. Carl Sandburg, the American poet commented: "Life is like an onion. You peel it off one layer at a time; and sometimes you weep."
• Glycemic load: 5

ORANGE: Most people think about vitamin C when talking about the health benefits of oranges, which they are rich in, but their benefits go well beyond vitamin C. They are a great source of fiber, thiamine, and folate, as well as potassium. Despite their high sugar content, they have a low glycemic load due to their rich content of polyphenols and fiber. Orange peels have many uses: may help to remove grease or oil spots; combine with warm water and spray in your vegetable garden to limit aphids and slugs.
• Glycemic load: 6

PAPAYA: Can work in a variety of dishes—salads, soups, sauces—both sweet and savory, and even sorbet. Great source of vitamins C and A, as well as fiber; can also be very beneficial for digestion. Even though it is a sugar-containing fruit, its glycemic load is low due to high water and phytonutrient content. If you run out of black pepper, grind the black seeds of the papaya fruit as an alternative.
• Glycemic load: 3

PEACH: A member of the stone fruit family, this fruit is native to Northwest China. Provides vitamin C and potassium. Due to its numerous nutrients but higher sugar content, peaches

should be added to other foods, such as salads, smoothies, or salsa to provide a sweet, fresh taste. With over 2,000 varieties, one of the ways to distinguish is by how the pit separates from the flesh of the fruit. Clingstone: not easily, and Freestone: easy separation.
• Glycemic Load: 5

PEAR: So many varieties, so little time. Can be crunchy or soft. Beneficial in its content of fiber, vitamin C, potassium, and copper. Make sure you eat the skin, as it contains most of its 6 gm of fiber, about 20 percent of the minimum recommended amount of fiber in a day. The peel also contains important molecules that support your health called quercetin and anthocyanins. Eat them raw, in a smoothie or salad. May roast or poach with herbs and spices. Goes nicely with pork or chicken.
• Glycemic load: 6

PEA: A good source of protein, about 8 gm per serving. High in fiber, folate, thiamine, vitamins A, C, K, and a host of other minerals. Easy to add to almost any dish and certainly worth it, seeing it is packed with nutrition. Peas were one of the first plants cultivated by humans and have remained a staple food source through the centuries.
• Glycemic load: 8

PINEAPPLE: Despite its relatively high sugar content, this fruit is packed with goodness, including high levels of vitamin C, potassium, and manganese. It has many beneficial compounds, especially bromelain, which can help the body in numerous ways, including assisting digestion. Pineapple has long been a fruit representing friendship and hospitality, often displayed on anything welcoming guests.
• Glycemic load: 36

PLUM: Generally grown as a yellow or red fruit, referred to as a stone fruit due to its central pit, has a good amount of vitamins A,

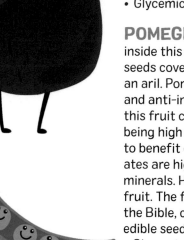

C, and K, copper, potassium, and fiber. Prunes, which are dried plums, also have health benefits, including easing constipation to improving cholesterol. Delicious eaten raw or in many different recipes. The second most cultivated fruit, coming in a variety of colors from white to purple, they are grown on every continent except Antarctica.
• Glycemic load: 5

POMEGRANATE: So much goodness inside this inedible skin. Hundreds of edible seeds covered by a juicy, sweet fruit known as an aril. Pomegranates are potent antioxidants and anti-inflammatories, two powerful ways this fruit contributes to health. And due to being high in nitrates, they have been shown to benefit exercise. Additionally, pomegranates are high in a wide range of vitamins and minerals. Hard to go wrong with this delicious fruit. The fruit, mentioned numerous times in the Bible, can have anywhere from 200–1,400 edible seeds.
• Glycemic load: 18

POTATO: We are all familiar with Mr. Potato Head, so I don't think potatoes need any introduction—certainly not in the way of french fries. However, it is very important to realize that most of the nutritional benefit (high in potassium, vitamin C, and B vitamins) is found in the skin, so please include this part of the potato while cooking. Potatoes also provide your gut bacteria something called resistant starch, especially when served cool. Red and smaller potatoes may provide more fiber and therefore lower glycemic load than the larger brown potato. This worldwide cultivated crop, introduced to the world by the conquering Spaniards, likely originated in the Andes, somewhere in the region of Peru or Bolivia. Each day, over a billion people—that's 1,000,000,000—eat potatoes, making them one of the most important crops worldwide.
• Glycemic load: 29

PRUNE: (See PLUM) These nutritionally beneficial dried plums also have a much longer shelf life. Consume prunes dried at lower temperatures to avoid any harmful chemicals. By using two means to relieve constipation, bulk forming in the form of fiber and osmotic in the form of the sugar sorbitol, prunes are very effective laxatives.
• Glycemic load: 5

PUMPKIN: Hopefully you have had a ton of fun carving pumpkins (perhaps even decorating your brother or sister with pumpkin pulp). Good news, you can consume the pulp and seeds of many pumpkin varieties, due to their high nutritious value. One of the foods containing high levels of vitamin A, it also contains vitamins B and C, as well as many minerals and phytonutrients. Referred to as pepitas or "little seed of the squash," pumpkins seeds provide additional health benefits including healthy fats and are high in minerals that can support bone health: magnesium, calcium, and potassium.
• Glycemic load: 3; seeds: 2

RADICCHIO: A healthy part of any diet, but often used in Mediterranean and Italian dishes. High in fiber, which is great for your gut, and high in vitamin K, which is beneficial to bone and brain health. You can certainly eat this leafy vegetable raw, but cooking it will mellow the bitter taste. In ancient times, the leaves were used for treating diarrhea, healing wounds, and maintaining heart health and blood sugars.
• Glycemic load: 1

RADISH: Another great, low-carb vegetable, packed with so much goodness to support your nutritional needs whether vegan or keto. And a bunch of different varieties to try, which are gaining in popularity due to their health benefits. Eaten raw they are somewhat spicy, cooked they provide an earthy, almost sweet taste. Enjoy this cruciferous vegetable packed with minerals,

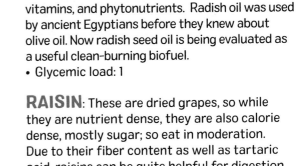

vitamins, and phytonutrients. Radish oil was used by ancient Egyptians before they knew about olive oil. Now radish seed oil is being evaluated as a useful clean-burning biofuel.
• Glycemic load: 1

RAISIN: These are dried grapes, so while they are nutrient dense, they are also calorie dense, mostly sugar; so eat in moderation. Due to their fiber content as well as tartaric acid, raisins can be quite helpful for digestion and having regular bowel movements. Boron, helpful for bones, wounds, and possibly brain health, is a mineral found in raisins. Again, please consider organic when possible. A staple at George Washington's dinner table when home at Mount Vernon, raisins have been cherished throughout history, even used as prizes during Roman and Greek sporting events.
• Glycemic load: 20

RUTABAGA: Considered a cross between a turnip and cabbage, these belong in the cruciferous family. They are an excellent source of vitamins B, C, E, potassium, magnesium, and calcium, as well as smaller amounts of phosphorus and selenium. Like other cruciferous vegetables, they contain glucosinolates which have been proven to be an excellent
support of health. With less of the carbohydrates, and more of the nutrients, rutabagas can be used in the kitchen in similar ways to potatoes.
• Glycemic load: 4

SPINACH: Inexpensive, easy to prepare, and considered a "superfood" due to its near completeness as a food source. Good for Popeye due to being rich in iron, but it is also a decent source of protein. High in vitamins A, C, and K, folate, as well as omega 3 fatty acids. If you are going to eat meat, especially grilled, consider adding some spinach, as its high chlorophyll content can block the damaging effects of heterocyclic amines.
• Glycemic load: 0

STRAWBERRY: Great for your skin and overall health. A good source of fiber, making up 26 percent of the fruit's carbohydrates. Also, strawberries provide significant amounts of vitamin C, and manganese, but they make a real difference in their antioxidant and phytonutrient makeup, helping to resist heart disease, lower blood sugar, and fight cancer. Fisetin, a molecule found in strawberries is a class of senolytics—found to help with fighting the effects of aging. Strawberry is a popular food flavoring, so be careful it is not an artificial substitute rather than the incredible real thing.
• Glycemic load: 3

TANGELO: A product of natural hybridization, between an orange and grapefruit. Like other citrus fruits, it too is high in vitamin C, but expect to get some other vitamins and minerals from eating this fruit, especially vitamin A and calcium. The flavinoids in tangelos add to their ability to fight disease. Delicious on their own or added to fruit or regular salads. The entire citrus fruit can be used for juice, syrups, marmalade, and oils.
• Glycemic load: 6

TOMATO: Rich in both vitamins and plant compounds, one known as lycopene which has been extensively studied for its health benefits. Note that most of these beneficial compounds are found in the skin of the ripened tomato, so don't discard when consuming. This is one food that should definitely be consumed locally, due to the sprays used to ripen the tomatoes shipped green and immature. So enjoy this delicious, juicy, sweet food in many different dishes. Botanically, tomatoes are fruits, grown from a flower with many seeds. As a culinary classification, they are vegetables.
• Glycemic load: 2

TURNIP: Turnips do not let the cruciferous vegetable family down. They too bring a variety of amazing phytonutrients, and antioxidants that have made this family a go-to for obtaining and maintaining health. Add the greens to the root vegetable for additional vitamins A, C, and K as well as tremendously beneficial nitrates. Historically, turnips have not been a complimentary vegetable: in Roman times it was hurled at unpopular figures, and in Charles Dickens's novels people considered idiots were referred to as turnips. In Ireland and Scotland, turnips are used to carve Halloween lanterns.
• Glycemic load: 3

UGLI FRUIT: An easy-to-peel cross between a grapefruit and orange, this tasty fruit has many health benefits. These include high sources of vitamins and minerals, especially vitamin C, as well as flavonoids such as naringenin which help fight disease. So don't be put off by its name or appearance, as this definitely should be added to your salads or fruit plate. Only being discovered about eighty years ago in Jamaica, this is still the country that produces the most amount of this delicious and nutritious fruit.
• Glycemic load: 4

WAKAME: Like most edible seaweeds, wakame has been associated with multiple health benefits. Wakame provides a moderate amount of beneficial nutrients. Additionally, it provides iodine, which is essential for normal thyroid production—just be careful not to eat too much. Add to salads as a leafy green or add to your favorite soup. May also be consumed dried as a snack. Ensure you are getting well-sourced wakame/seaweeds, as they may contain heavy metals or pollutants—fortunately, studies suggest this may be quite low.
• Glycemic load: 1

WATERMELON: A wonderfully fresh, sweet, and refreshing fruit, to be enjoyed at any time but certainly during the summer. Also provides a good amount of water, and is quite low in calories. I love this fruit because it is a rich

source of citrulline, a precursor to nitric oxide, which is a very important molecule in the body. It is also very high in lycopene, which also has some tremendous health benefits. This all makes up for it not being very high in antioxidants, but does provide some vitamin C and copper, which is not very high in the Western diet. Perfectly named, watermelon is 92 percent water by content. Also, consider eating the entire fruit, as it is around the world—the rinds are stir-fried, stewed, or pickled, and the seeds are roasted similar to pumpkin seeds.
• Glycemic load: 3

YAM: Not quite as sweet as sweet potatoes, but just as versatile in the kitchen, packed with a good array of nutrients, minerals, and fiber. The resistant starch in these tubers can be helpful in building healthy bacteria and possibly even weight loss. The word "yam," believed to have derived from some West African languages, means "to eat."
• Glycemic load: 18

YUCA: Not to be confused with yucca, which is more of an ornamental plant used for its medicinal value, yuca is a root vegetable from the cassava plant. For vegans or vegetarians, this is a great source of choline, B and C vitamins, as well as an array of other vitamins. Not so much for our Keto friends—due to the high carbohydrate content. Due to an easily removed or degraded toxin, yuca should not be consumed raw.
• Glycemic load: 41

ZUCCHINI: Part of the gourd family, zucchini and its relative squash can be an excellent, more nutritious, alternative to pasta (search zucchini or squash noodles recipes on the web). Easy to grow and high in antioxidants, phytonutrients, and vitamins, zucchini is a must-have in your summer vegetable garden. Botanically more like a fruit, but very much a vegetable in cookery; you can harvest this about forty-five to sixty days after planting.
• Glycemic load: 2

FUN RECIPES using fruits and veggies

EDAMAME **AND** ESCAROLE **SOUP**

Ingredients:
1 bunch escarole or other bitter leafed greens
  washed and chopped into 2 inch chunks.
1/4 cup fat (butter, olive oil, or coconut oil)
1 medium onion finely chopped
1 tsp sea salt
3 cloves garlic peeled and crushed/minced
2 cups edamame shelled fresh or frozen
4 cups vegetable stock
1 cup soy milk or cream
1/2 cup goat cheese or feta cheese (optional)

Directions:
· Preheat oven to 425° F. On a large baking sheet, spread
  butter on the pan. Spread escarole on the sheet and
  drizzle 1 tablespoon melted butter or other fat on top
  of escarole. Roast for 18–20 minutes, stirring halfway
  through. Set aside.
· Meanwhile, in a large saucepan over medium heat, sauté
  onion and garlic in remaining 3 tablespoons fat until
  tender, about 5–7 minutes. Add edamame and vegetable stock. Bring to a boil, cover, and reduce heat to low.
  Simmer over low heat until edamame is very tender,
  about 20 minutes.
· Carefully transfer roasted escarole and the edamame
  mixture (with liquid) to a large food processor or blend-
  er, working in batches, if necessary. Process the mixture
  until puréed. Add organic soy milk (or cream), cheese,
  and salt. Process until very smooth.
· Serve soup immediately or reheat in saucepan over low
  heat until desired temperature is reached.

UPLAND CRESS **AND** UGLI FRUIT **SUMMER SALAD**

Ingredients:
2 bunches upland cress leaves (or watercress if you can't
  find it), and attached tender stems only
1 ugli fruit, supremed (segmented and all membrane
  removed).
  Substitute grapefruit if needed
1 orange, supremed
1/4 cup orange juice
2 tbs extra-virgin olive oil
Sea salt and freshly ground black pepper

Directions:
· Mix orange juice, salt, pepper, and olive oil in a jar.
· Toss with water cress and top with ugli fruit and
  oranges.

ICEBERG WEDGE **WITH** INDIAN MANGOS

Dressing Ingredients:
1/2 cup olive oil
1/2 cup mango juice. I like mango nectar because it's a
    little thicker
1/4 cup of lemon juice
2 tablespoons of fresh chopped cilantro
1/2 tsp of salt
1/4 tsp of pepper

- Blend in a mixer and use on salad.
- If serving to adults add a 1/4 cup of flaked red pepper
  for some spice and put some dried jalapeño slices on
  top of the salad for some crunch.

Salad Ingredients:
Iceberg lettuce head
Indian mango (smaller and more yellowish/green skin,
    these are a little less sweet than their larger red cousins)
8 pieces cooked bacon
2 ounces blue cheese crumbles
1 small red onion
16-20 grape tomatoes

Directions:
- Cook bacon and drain on paper towels. and when cool
  crunch into pieces.
- Cut mango into small squares by halving it first and
  separating sides from center seed. Cut the squares
  inside the skin and then flip inside out and scrape the
  squares into a bowl.
- Slice red onion very thinly, set aside.
- Cut head of iceberg into four wedges, remove the core,
  and plate. On each wedge sprinkle 1/4 of the onion slices, 1/4 of the bacon crumbles, 4 or 5 grape tomatoes,
  and 1/4 of the mango squares.
- Drizzle with the dressing, top
  with blue cheese crumbles
  and ENJOY!

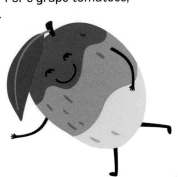

ROASTED ASPARAGUS **AND** APPLES

Apple's ingredients:
6 crisp apples (Granny Smith, Jonagold, Honey Crisp or
    whatever apple you prefer)
1/8 cup cinnamon
1/4 cup brown sugar
Pinch sea salt
1 tbs softened butter

Directions:
- Core apples and chop into bite-sized pieces. Mix cinnamon, salt, and sugar together, and toss chopped apples
  in cinnamon/sugar mix.
- Pour coated apples into buttered roasting dish.
- Bake at 400° F for 30-35 minutes toss and stir once
  after 15 minutes, watch for burning.
- Serve with roasted asparagus and if you have leftovers
  eat with yogurt or oatmeal the next day.

Asparagus ingredients:
2 bunches fresh asparagus
1/4 cup grapeseed oil or coconut oil
Garlic salt (I like the kind with parsley flakes)

Directions:
- Spray oil (you can make your own with a small spray
  bottle, you have to clean out the sprayer every so often).
- Wash asparagus and snap off the bottoms.
- Spread one level of asparagus on a large cookie sheet
  sprayed with oil then drizzle with oil. Sprinkle with garlic
  salt. If you do not like soggy asparagus be careful not to
  drench the spears with oil.
- Roast at 400° F for 30
  minutes checking often
  and turning. I like my spears
  brown and crispy so I leave
  mine in a few minutes longer.
  Take out of the oven when
  they have the desired ten-
  derness and eat with roasted
  apples.

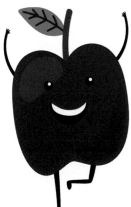

ROASTED OKRA WITH ORANGE BALSAMIC REDUCTION

Ingredients:
2 pounds fresh whole okra sliced in half lengthwise
¼ cup grapeseed or coconut oil
½ cup balsamic vinegar
2 tbs maple syrup
2 large oranges
1 small onion
Garlic salt to taste (I like the kind with parsley flakes in it)

Directions:
- Pre-heat oven to 400° F.
- Zest both oranges and put zest aside. Juice oranges (or substitute 1/4 cup orange juice) and mix in a sauce pan with balsamic vinegar and maple syrup.
- Cover baking sheet with oil, reserve some to top the okra.
- Place okra on the sheet seed side down, drizzle remaining oil on the okra, and sprinkle with garlic salt.
- Roast in oven 15 minutes.

While the okra roasts:
- Heat balsamic, juice, and maple syrup mixture over medium heat until it bubbles then lower the heat until it reaches desired consistency. If you let it heat on high for too long it will become too thick to pour. Stir the mixture often to prevent sticking or over cooking. Once it has thickened, remove from heat, and let it sit. Mix in 1/2 of the orange zest.
- Remove okra from the oven, place on a serving dish, drizzle with balsamic reduction, and sprinkle with remaining orange zest. Serve immediately.

FUN FACTS

https://www.medicalnewstoday.com/articles/282769

https://www.healthline.com/nutrition

https://foodrevolution.org/

https://fruitsandveggies.org/

https://www.verywellfit.com/

http://justfunfacts.com/

https://crafty.house/

https://www.softschools.com/

https://foodprint.org/real-food/edamame/

https://www.thekitchn.com/cranberries-212847

SELF Nutrition Data | Food Facts, Information & Calorie Calculator, https://www.appleholler.com/orchard-farm/all-about-apples/apple-fun-facts/

Home - Mayo Clinic Health System, https://facts.net/lifestyle/food/food-facts

https://www.mentalfloss.com/article/63100/11-things-you-might-not-have-known-about-garlic

https://www.rockefellerfoundation.org/wp-content/uploads/2021/07/True-Cost-of-Food-Full-Report-Final.pdf

D. Aune, E. Giovannucci, P. Boffetta, L. T. Fadnes, N. Keum, T. Norat, et al. "Fruit and vegetable intake and the risk of cardiovascular disease, total cancer and all-cause mortality – a systematic review and dose-response meta-analysis of prospective studies," Int J Epidemiol 2017, 46:1029–56.

L. Chatzi, G. Apostolaki, I. Bibakis, et al. "Protective effect of fruits, vegetables and the Mediterranean diet on asthma and allergies among children in Crete," Thorax 2007, 62:677–83.

William T. Clements, Sang-Rok Lee, and Richard J. Bloomer, "Nitrate Ingestion: A Review of the Health and Physical Performance Effects," Nutrients, November 2014, 6(11): 5224–64.

H. C. Hung, K. J. Joshipura, R. Jiang, F. B. Hu., D. Hunter, S. A. Smith-Warner, "Fruit and vegetable intake and risk of major chronic disease," Journal of the National Cancer Institute, 2004, 96:1577–84.

Nagisa Mori, et al. "Cruciferous vegetable intake and mortality in middle-aged adults: A prospective cohort study," Clin Nutr, April 2019, 38(2):631–43.

Dong Wang, et al. "Fruit and vegetable intake and morbidity," Circulation, March 2021, 143 (17): 1642–54.

You Can Help Your Body's Cells!

These cells are made stronger when you eat enough of the right foods!

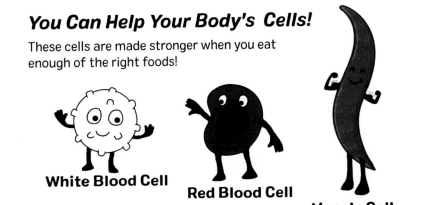

White Blood Cell

Red Blood Cell

Muscle Cell

Fruit or Vegetable?

Can you tell which is which? They are identified by either an orange or green bubble throughout the book.

fruit

vegetable